Oct. 1989 Marilyn Wagenius

AF864166

IN TRANSIT

IN TRANSIT

By

JANET BALDWIN ZIEGELE

Illustrated by Ginnie Porter

YE GALLEON PRESS
FAIRFIELD, WASHINGTON

Library of Congress Cataloging-in-Publication Data

Ziegele, Janet Baldwin, 1917-1988
In transit / by Janet Baldwin Ziegele: illustrated by Ginnie Porter.
p. cm.
I. Title.
PS3576.128715 1989 89-22420 811'.54--dc20
ISBN 0-87770-474-0

DEDICATION

Photo by: Neal Evarts

This book is published in memory of the author, Janet Baldwin Ziegele (1917-1988) by the people in her life who loved her most, her husband, two daughters and son.

Dedicated teacher, librarian, journalist, poet, wife and mother, she always found time for us and was always there when we needed her.

TABLE OF CONTENTS

GOING HOME

Scatter my ashes on the hills of Montana
Ride a young horse who knows nothing of death,
Catch the brisk breeze that sweeps down through the coulees
And let it transport me away on its breath.

Then I can still celebrate Nature's wild seasons
Until the last day when we all must depart;
The trumpet will call me from some flowery meadow
With the breath of Montana still warm on my heart.

GP

ENCOUNTER

Grief, you are no stranger now.
You used to peek around the corners of my youth
Like a dark mortician, waiting to preside
When dolls were lost or kittens died.
But now I know the fury of your face
As you weaken my defenses in funereal embrace.
And victory, if won, has left me victim of my loss.
Ever in retreat, you lurk in dreams and wait
To stab me once again with memory
Before I move beyond your realm of pain
Into the calm mainstream of life again.

REINCARNATION

Must I return to Earth again?
To be a prisoner of genes and chromosomes,
Or a victim of the strange dichotomies of love?
Where in the teeming multitudes
Is there a sanctuary for the private soul?
To live again is to endure the forces that erode
A spirit needing to be free.

But how can I deny the renaissance of spring
That creates life anew from ancient roots
And dangles promises of wonderment to come
Reminding me that Earth is beautiful
And heaven once more just within my grasp.
With youth to challenge all of the beginnings
And love to lead me gently by the hand.

KARMA

I think I must have been a Buddhist monk
In some life long ago that lingers still.
I've learned the limits of desire, the pain
Of life that battles with the will
To seek the going-out-of-fire. The changing form
Of currents merging in the abiding stream
Create familiar patterns as they flow;
The flame, its parts consumed to make the gleam.
I yield to life, still searching for that calm,
The seeds of karma surely all are sown.
But the imp of ego wakes and doubt intrudes--
I'd rather be the hammer than the stone.

GENESIS

'Tis the leaving that I'd mind,
Nothing to pack and no time for goodbyes.
I'd like to look upon this home again
Before I drift once more into the unknown sea
Where learning and forgetting are the tides
That wash old memories away and consecrate
The soul for its rebirth.
So much of hard-earned knowledge must be lost--
The long apprenticeship to love and art--
Then once again the pain of parturition.
Endings and beginnings, born in tears,
Into the white light of God's eternity.

HOME FIRES

When I was young the spirits in the wind
Would whistle catcalls from the corners of the earth.
It's all out there, the siren voices moan
As the rafters shake and tumbleweeds
Flee from the howling demons of the storm.
The fire within the ancient stove is warm,
But warmer still is youth's desire to fly
Before the winds, outracing yet pursuing,
Confident as only youth can be,
That reality is somewhere in the dream.
Wisdom is bought with precious coins,
Tossed to appease the storms
And find the road that leads
Back to the ancient hearth fire.

THE SEARCH FOR YESTERDAY

The boards lie silvered in the sun,
Scattered thinly over crumbled footings,
Disguising well the boundaries
That once embraced the living souls
Who called it home. A caprice of time
Or careless fortune pushed those lives
With gentle nudgings toward a final anonymity.
Sad, momentous questions hover
Over silvered boards and souls.
Somewhere there are voiceless echoes,
Untapped memories and faded faces
Are there waiting in the shadows with the key--
The elusive legacy of words.

OCTOBER

A mad magician came today
  (he's often called October)
And reached into his bag of tricks,
  declaring green too sober,
He turned the maple tree to gold--
  then proceeded to disrobe her!
She watched her leaves fall in dismay,
  distressed to see them go.
Don't worry, said the madman
  as he hustled to and fro.
He conjured up a wintry blast
  and draped her limbs with snow!

PRELUDE

I walk to meet the Autumn
As the leaves begin to fall,
Their gold so generously spent
Makes beggars of us all.

If I could keep October's glow
For warmth when nights grow cold,
I'd welcome metamorphosis
And laugh at growing old.

CHILD OF THE UNIVERSE

I reach out to the universe, spinning, spinning,
To the network of space which generates me.
I am but a spark, an atom of being,
A part of an electrical, vast cosmic sea.
A miniscule ganglion pulsing with life
Tapping the force of a magnetic earth,
I cling to the magic of fragile existence
And glow from the energy kindled at birth.
For I still am one with the earth and the heavens,
I move with the tides, and I yearn for the light,
So much to be done while my star is still shining
Before it blinks out in the darkness of night.

THE JOURNEY

We came to see you in the Autumn
Climbing to the high pass and dropping down,
To the Silver Valley bathed in golden light
From the candleglow of tamarack in the sun.
The birches trembled, setting their bright doubloons
Aglitter like Christmas ornaments of filigree,
And the mountain ash shone red with promises
To the birds in wintertime,
Such a journey must have a glorious destination.
And so it did. Our children waited there.

SNOWBOUND

I really loved you, Autumn, and
I begged you not to leave me to the ravages of Winter.
Let's live together where the winds are kind, I said,
And sunlight is a sensuous acolyte.
But one morning you were gone, and my ardent phrases faltered
As I watched a snowflake fall, and then another, softly,
Subtly draping the brown woods left desolate by your desertion.
Winter, clever rogue, approaches in the guise of lover,
Shyly showing off the frost-rimmed tracery of lilac branches,
And like an ancient sorcerer, reflects their likeness of my windowpane.
He knows my first admiring glance will blossom into passion
When he reveals the city lights, a-shimmer 'neath a rosy mountain
In the dying sunset's glow. I'm spellbound in a snowbound world.
And yet I know his alter ego will emerge and challenge me
To deathdance on the paths where ice and snow
Lie over April's blooms. How soon I see his mud-stained robes
And wonder where the magic went. His wintry, wind-snarled locks
Have cooled the flame that beauty fanned, and left my fickle heart
Awash with longing for the arms of Spring.

AUTUMN DÉJÀ VU

I know you, Indian summer,
With your wily Autumn ways.
You woo me with your golden touch
And poignant violet days.
That sweetly melancholy charm
Has won my heart before--
Another life, another time,
Perhaps another shore.
Your misty wistful magic
Will always claim the part
That's hidden from the world's regard--
My still romantic heart.

WINTER STANDOFF

I hate to see old Winter come again
With his chill announcement that the summer's gone.
He blows away the gold of autumn leaves
And piles them on my doorstep and my lawn.
Untidy soul, he hovers as they fly
And grimly watches summer's finery go,
Until the colors fade and disappear,
And then he spreads his cold white cloak of snow.
Oh, I should find some beauty in this scene,
But actually there isn't much to cheer
When Winter gilds my hair with frosty white
And smirks, "I've only added one more year."
But I have battled Winter's woes before,
So I conspire with timeless Mother Earth
And plant some hyacinths and daffodils
And wait for springtime's glorious rebirth.

A CANDLE BURNING

Autumn steals upon the land,
  touching the countryside with Midas fingers.
The solemn pines and fir,
  wrapped in pyramidal dignity,
    disdain all change,
But far below the birch and ash tremble with color
  and risk their all for one golden shimmering moment
    in the sun.
They stand like candles burning,
  consumed by beauty — promising immortality.

LORETTA

She left us as a petal falls,
No need to speak again,
Her message had been told so well
Through years of service when
She shared her gift with all who came
To stand at learning's door.
She spoke with gentleness and grace
And left us richer than before.
We'll miss you, dear Loretta,
But our loss is Heaven's gain
Your gentle ghost will bless us
And your lessons will remain.

CARNIVAL

I hope that if I must grow old
I'll still like Ferris wheels
And listen with the same delight
To derbied barkers' spiels
As I do now.

I hope the India rubber man
Will fascinate me then,
And may my blood be chilled once more
By Borneo's wild men
As it is now.

But just in case I grow too old
And listen with a frown
To tinkling of calliopes
When carnivals reach town--
I'll just go now.

1938 or 1939

MARS' SOLILOQUY

I hear the tread of stamping feet
That echo on with steady beat
Those little men go off to war
And spill their blood on a foreign shore.

I laugh with glee at the cannon's roar
And slyly watch the airplanes soar
And with one disapproving hand
Sweep their crumpled wings to land.

With a rumbling laugh that shakes the seas
And makes a tempest of the breeze
I toss the menacing submarine
And make a chaos of the scene.

I am a king whose magic thrills
And grasps the power of strong men's wills
And with the lure of a trumpet call
I watch the youth of a nation fall.

1938 or 1939

THE THREE BUTTES

Three buttes stand out upon the skyline
Marking one far boundary of my childhood world.
The sun in winter rose behind them,
Casting reluctant, meager shadows
Across the dry Montana earth.
Even in spring the land did not give freely,
But held its young grass
Close against the tough rock-crusted hills.
Yet within each blade was locked the power
To make strong lambs and calves.
The buttes stood sentinel against the world,
Immune alike to suffering and to joy.
The battle made them strong; they learned that drought and hail
Were temporary devils, perhaps next spring
Will offer one more chance.
The buttes remain, a landmark in my life,
Telling me that this is home,
Where life is difficult, and yet
The good things are there waiting to be won.

JENNY

I said goodbye to Jenny
When the winds were blowing chill
Across the sad Wyoming prairie.
I can feel our sorrow still
As I watched our five young children
(And another home new-born)
Huddle close. How could she leave us,
Broken-hearted and forlorn?
Oh, many years have passed since then,
We learned to live each day,
But the laughter and the music stopped
When Jenny went away.

WILLIE AND JANET

My grandparents danced on the Wyoming prairie
As the fiddler warmed up with a "promenade all."
The firelight shone bright on their handsome young faces
And their cares were forgotten in the gay music's thrall.
Their children watched rapt from the shadowy sidelines,
This memory imprinted, forever to glow
As Mama and Papa danced gaily together
When life held no sadness on those nights long ago.
That scene was a talisman held by their children.
Whenever fate's buffets would leave them forlorn,
They remembered the love that surrounded their childhood--
And warmed generations yet to be born.

EARLY SETTLERS

They came from wornout cities
or little villages with narrow men,
looking for a sky that flows forever,
inviting all to breathe without constraint.
They sought the uplands or the prairies
where the distant skyline hovered,
testing manhood, faith and vision
as their eyes defined new bounds.
Such were the pioneers who dared
to grasp the golden ring and swing
in wild parabola into a strange new land,
a land now mellowed and familiar,
patterned by their struggles and
the footsteps of their children
into a place called home.

SOUTH DAKOTA SUNSET

The glow of Indian campfires
Still stain the western sky
Across the twilit miles
To jagged peaks that haven't changed
Since Red Cloud and Sitting Bull
Challenged the white man's destiny
And lost their hunting grounds.
Their spirits haunt the sunset
And the echoes of their war cries
Fade away into the lonesome night
Where wailing women wait.
The victors mined the gold
And flung their freeway ribbons
Across the green Dakota hills.
To tempt the tourist tide,
Crushing the old buffalo bones
Into the primeval dust of dinosaurs.

NOCTURNE

Blue mountains under twilight's spell,
A world soft-veiled in pink pastel
Of evening sky. An errant cloud
That passing by, reflects the soft gold
Of the sun, and whispers softly,
"Day is done."

1938 or 1939

CATALDO

Traffic scuttles by on the Interstate below
failing to disturb the timeless dignity
of the mission on the knoll. It stands,
inscrutable as the Indians who carved
its timbers from the forest, working
shoulder to shoulder with the priests.
The Black Robes cast their net
and brought the tribes within its folds,
where peace ruled for a moment
in the community of man.

SWEET LIBERTY

The rockets flare across the sky
In the warm midsummer night
Thrilling children of all ages
With their brilliant bursts of light.
We celebrate our liberty
With a carefree show of war,
Wrest beauty from the anguish
Felt by those who live no more.
Brave words by Patrick Henry
And the deeds of Nathan Hale
Served freedom's cause at birthing
Let's attend her progress well.
Enjoy her gifts, but don't abuse
The rights we hold so fast.
Defend her for our children's sake
Our legacy from the past.

CROSS ROADS

Walk softly past the ancient shrines
  that mark the crossroads where the demons wait
    to catch the simple traveler unaware.
Look sharp across the network of invisible crossroads
  where long ago the trails were worn
    where men made choices locked in destiny.
The steps of conquerors have traced these ways,
  now haunted by old battles, old decisions,
    and the aftermath of inhumanity.
Signposts flourish in ambiguous design
  like missiles poised for flight
    across the unseen lines of longitude
      waiting to devastate the certainties of life.
Walk softly!

BEYOND TOMORROW

There's a better world tomorrow
When the dust bowl is no more,
Said the voices of the Thirties
When the wolf was at the door.
But the Forties brought a dreadful war
Through which our nation bled,
And the commies of the Fifties
Made us look beneath our bed.
The Sixties were a shocker
As we saw our leaders shot,
And Vietnam was so shameful
That the country turned to pot.
The voices of the Seventies
All shouted loudly "ME!"
Women, babies, everyone
All wanted to be free.
Oh, is there peace beyond tomorrow
Unplagued by war and woe?
If only Heaven offers it,
I think we all should go.

STEPPING STONES

Daring the oceans, taming the land,
Bearing the children, determined to stand
Where the hand of oppression no longer can bruise
The proud spirit of freedom too precious to lose.
Building the cabins, building the schools,
Building the churches, creating the tools
To build for tomorrow a life that is free
Of all burdensome chores through technology.
This life we enjoy we inherit from those
Who laid stepping stones — from their labors we rose
To become masters, not slaves, free to work or to play.
Let us cherish those efforts and keep building today.

THE QUEST

My ancestors lived here
Though now there is no vestige of their passing.
I look to find the imprint of their lives
But see no shadow from the past upon the living tide,
No cairn upon the hilltop
Or echo from the cadence of their days.
The environment of Earth was cradle
To the dream of their existence,
But they are gone and condos rise
From the dust of their log cabins.
How can I speak with them?
Perhaps it is enough that I should stand,
Inheritor of all their dreams,
And look not to the past, but to the road ahead,
And leave my fragile mark upon this land
That always will be home.

MIND POWER

I'm going to go and live in my head.
I'm tired of this constant fuss
about Arabs and gun runners,
   people who lie,
      false prophets and terrorists,
         pie in the sky,
and mothers who are mostly unwed.
I'll think about good things instead,
like babies and lollipops,
   people who smile,
      the givers and helpers
         unburdened by guile.
Friends who are cheerful,
   old memories fed
by the dreams that still live in my head.

BLUE SKIES

Blue skies, playing hide-and-seek
behind gray clouds
weeping raindrops
washing winter's cast-offs
into gutters,
a needed ablution
for frigid lacerations.
Clouds, retreating from the sun,
at last admit blue skies
and herald new beginnings.

GP

HAIKU

The mist rests lightly
on the mountaintop--
A signal puff
Of gray smoke.

Bare branches reach
toward the sky,
kept warm by
An Eiderdown of snow.

Himalayas, Pyrenees--
No, only snow
In drifts upon
My deck.

THE EMPTY NEST

The house is silent now,
Its battlements secure.
The radio fills the corners
Where the children's voices were.
The fingerprints are gone,
No toys on the floor--
But I'd gladly trade this precious peace
To have them home once more.

WHAT'S IN A NAME?

If I were named Mary
I know that I'd be
A person much different
Than little old me.

A model of virtue,
And beauty, of course,
She never would look
like she fell from her horse.

I might rant and holler
And even be mean,
But Mary would always
Be calm and serene.

It's funny the difference
A name can convey.
If my parents had known this,
I'd be famous today.

CREATION

When God looked out on His blue-green world
At the dawn of the seventh day,
The fiery dusts of creation had stilled
And a gentle breeze carried them away.

The angels looked down and were truly amazed.
"It's just like Heaven!" they cried.
The song of their joy on the crystalline air
Was a great melodious tide.

As the music washed over the newborn earth
In the light of the glorious morn,
God gently blew life in the formless clay
And the soul of man was born.

"To inherit this marvelous, wonderful world
You must love one another," He said,
"And touch not of the fruit that the devil
Has placed here over your head."

"To inherit the earth! What an opportune gift,"
Man cried, as he reached for the fruit
Of the only forbidden tree in this land--
And the devil got his first recruit.

"You've forgotten a place for the sinners, I see,"
Smirked Satan in false dismay.
"You used up all the primordial dust
When you gave them those feet of clay."

God thought, then said, "Maybe a place isn't quite
What rebellious earth children require."
"There are still some flames burning," said Satan,
"Let me fix up a sulphurous fire."

"No, these mortals must learn to love and obey--
Their spirits are partly divine.
They must live on this earth, even yearn to be free,
But only their hearts can confine.

The most miserable souls will never know truth,
Will be deaf to life's melodies,
And the glorious world of beauty and love
May never reach sinners like these.

"Yet redemption is simple," said God. "The whole world
Can become like the Heaven above,
And peace rule forever, if only these fools
Can discover the meaning of love."

20 — 20

If I had x-ray eyes, I would seek elusive answers,
Probing soft subliminal corners where the lost dreams lie,
Exploring banished signs that say "Turn here" or "Go,"
Destinations never known, yet their presence whispers questions
In anxious decibels that echo in the attic of my mind.

Now I feel my eyes aglitter, though my ears can hear no trace
Of that once insistent clamor, as I look into the corners
Where the lost dreams were. Dazzled and awakened,
I see a golden treasure--incandescent memories
Of the years that came between. No room for past regrets here,
Precious moments speak no secrets, and my vision needs no puppet
To define its boundaries.

THE FRAGILE CUP

Country people love the sky
  and live in its embrace.
The children watch cloud castles merge
  and drift off into space.
The grandeur of a summer storm
  or streamers gold at dawn--
Kaleidoscope of colors, all
  so good to look upon.
But what will happen to our earth
  when smoke and poisons pour
And dim the crystal atmosphere
  so we can see no more?
The fragile cup so beautiful
  will shatter, and we'll lie
Amid the shards of man's conceit
  and watch our planet die.

THE ENEMY

I know you're out there.
I can see where you have chewed your way across the forests.
And laid a worm trail of cement across our farms.
Your dragon puffs of smoke obscure the sunlight
And threaten us with poison from the skies.
What kind of monster are you?
I think I would prefer to fight old Grendel,
His menace circumscribed by myth,
Than meet this faceless creature of today
In combat with no armor, only words.
Defeat will turn us back into the cave where our poor human bones
Will join our ancient cousin, Tyrannosaurus Rex,
Who also found this hostile world unfit.

WHAT'S IN STORE FOR '84

A look into the crystal ball
Might show us there's no world at all.
But then, of course, if we weren't here
There'd be no ball in which to peer.
So, let's assume the status quo
Prevails, with just the usual woe.
Brace up — are you in good condition
To listen to each politician
Tell why, in endless oratory,
A vote for him will lead to glory?
When he looks in his crystal ball
He says, "Our problems could be small--
We'll atomize the national debt
And then we'll have no deficit.
The money that we've saved we'll spend
To teach the young to comprehend.
We'll save the COLA's, feed the poor..."
Oh, politics is such a bore!
That hot air dims my crystal ball,
And now it isn't clear at all.
If this old world makes any sense
It takes far more intelligence
Than I can ever hope to score--
You tell *me* what's in '84

THREE, TWO, ONE...

Each generation past has had its share
Of prophets shouting "Doom! Prepare yourselves!
The day is soon to come when all must stand
While Armageddon's armies sweep the land."

Those seers grew old and others took their place,
Still telling of an incandescent end
For this, our home. A distant Judgment Day.
Some laughed, "We've heard all this before," said they.

But now at last we see the shape of Fate--
A wicked genie from the lamp of Man
It towers above us with his glove thrown down
And mankind trembles helpless 'neath his frown.

The seers' and prophets' words were proven true,
But all their wisdom now cannot avail
Nor stop the steady countdown as man tries
To get along with man before he dies.

MARS ASCENDANT

Take away your sacrificial lamb,
Your dancing maidens and your golden ram.
It's far too late for pretty sacrifice.
Old Jupiter might think such things are nice,
And once I might have settled for much less--
A country, maybe, or a wilderness.
But now I travel on a mushroom cloud
And friendly little games are not allowed.
So, if you want to play, the stakes are high,
And if you do not win--then you must die!

LACE

An embellishment of Nature
Borrowing the ripple from the running stream
And the imprint of the gull against the sky,
Tying visual lines into the fragile fabric.
As the spider weaves, so man creates his art
And spins the images that please the eye
Into a form so tangible we wear
It proudly to enhance our charms
Transforming each pretty girl into a queen.

LANTERNS

Look!
The pale
light reaches
out to touch the
night.

Come.
The day
awaits the
lazy child who
sleeps.

See
the gold
and orange
blossoms of the
light.

RUSSIAN ROULETTE

When you go to the store for a bottle of pills,
Do you hesitate as you decide?
How can you know that the package you pick
Is not laced with pure cyanide?
So your life was secure, and you felt no great risk
When you bought that new car, I suppose.
There were twenty new models awaiting your choice--
Is that lemon the one that you chose?
Life's full of the choices we make every day,
And most are a pretty safe bet,
But you're caught with the smoking gun hot in your hand
When you reach for your next cigarette.

SONNET FOR SAINT VALENTINE

A tribute to the patron saint of love
Who walked this earth so many years ago.
Did he show love in ways that now we know,
Or was his worship sent to One above,
All earthly passion just a thread thereof,
That lingered faintly in emotion's glow
Like lamplight from a dimly lit window
As Valentine sent aves to his love.

Oh, martyred saint, your message still is clear
Although your vows were of a different cast.
We still send valentines to those held dear
And hope that love will be returned at last.
Our martyrdom of love is eased therefore
By little missals bought in a drug store.

WORDS

My words are lost before the vibrations die
    and fall into the cacophanous pool
        of many voices striving to be heard.

I hastily retrieve their echoes
    and place the syllables on paper,
        changing them from liquid to a cryptographic scrawl
            that begs for brilliance.

Shaking out the platitudes, I arrange them carefully
    and warm them in the glow of a thousand footlights.
        Let the actors take my words and hang them out
            to leap and cavort in the winds of rhetoric,
                translating them once again into the language
                    of emotion from whence they came.

STUDY HOUR

My books are all in front of me
In definite alignment.
I grasp my pen and settle down
to do my Comp assignment.

Elusive thoughts go flitting by
Like moonlight on the sea
But dreams like this can't long endure
For I have my roommates three.

I grasp my hair and not my pen
I must ignore this din.
Ah, now a knock upon the door!
They all yell "Well, come in."

And when this visitor has gone
Another takes her place
They sing with unrestrained joy
Soprano, alto, bass.

The trio goes into decline
A bell rings loud and free.
They all dash madly to the phone
And holler in "Quad B."

So finally I give up hope
And thank the powers that be
That I am lucky to have not
Been cursed with more than three.

1938 or 1939

TRAVELOGUE

The wanderlust has lured me
And I know that I must go
To see the Aztec ruins
'Neath the skies of Mexico.

Or ship aboard a steamer
That is off to far Bombay
Or maybe one to China
And points westward in Cathay.

The Parthenon has called me
And castles on the Rhine.
The moonlight on the Taj Mahal
Is said to be divine.

The pyramids of Egypt
Will hail another land,
And farther still across the world
I may reach Samarkand.

On the heights of Mount Parnassus
In communion with the Muse
I'll find a blessed quiet
Which my heart will never lose.

The temples built to Venus
I hope to look upon
And I will see past warriors
On the plains of Marathon.

Ho for the southern pampas
Where the flowers never freeze
And I'll climb the mighty mountains
To the Christ of the Andes.

But now I must be patient
Draw up an easy chair
And open up a favorite book
To find contentment there.

1938

REVERIE

I dream of Egypt and the Nile,
And in my scene, a crocodile--
A camel with his timeless walk--
The Sphinx, that image made of rock--
An Arab chief, and tents of white--
Soft whispers on a sultry night--
Some hieroglyphics carved on stone--
A piece of prehistoric bone--
A desert sun o'er waves of sand--
My heart is longing for that land.
For winter here is so much colder--
Why did I read that travel folder?

1938

NIGHT ON THE TOWN

The freeway beckons straight ahead
Its geometric markers promising the nearness of the city,
And indeed the buildings rise
And the neatly bordered lawns give way
To more pretentious structures.
Neon lights shine out
Like bright fluorescent flowers
Proclaiming all the virtues
Of the food and dancing girls.
Their offerings far exceed
The pleasures of the ancient kings.
How long before our appetites are surfeited,
Our senses dulled by excess ostentation?
The journey back is to a quiet land
Where the moon reigns supreme
And the stars shine.

A LAKE BY ANY OTHER NAME

In a town filled with issues that are mostly mundane
The natives now argue about Lake Coeur d'Alene.
Is it better, they ask, for simplicity's sake
To refer to their jewel as Coeur d'Alene Lake?
But lovers of euphony say it's insane
To think of debasing their Lake Coeur d'Alene.
No weightier issue could capture the press
Than a small journalistic attempt to finesse.
In an age where good trivia cannot be ignored
Doug Clark is a winner — once more he has scored.
But if you really want readers to reach for their phone
Suggest that we label it "Lake Hagadone."

IDENTITY CRISIS

How many camels that you know
Would rather be a buffalo?
Do snakes rise up and hiss a wish
That they would love to be a fish?
Homo sapiens, it would seem,
Lack that vital self-esteem.
Instead they look at other men
And think they'd rather be Sean Penn.
The ladies, too, can't stay as is
They'd rather look like Cher or Liz.
Why not be glad that we're unique
And learn to live with our physique?
Our humanness gives us a plus--
How wonderful to be just us!

I FORGOT

Limerick

There was a young lady who sought
All her life to hit on a jackpot
But she won so much jack
Her accountants lost track
So she told the IRS "I forgot."

Couplet

When life unties the lover's knot
The saddest words are "I forgot."

LIMERICKS

There was a professor from Yale
Whose thesis was ordered by mail.
    It was so erudite
    That when asked to recite,
He stammered, "Well, it was on sale!"

A lottery winner named Bill
Said he almost passed out with the thrill.
    With ticket in hand
    He walked up to the stand
And swallowed it instead of his pill.

There was an old cowboy named Paul
Who spoke with a Montana drawl.
    Just give me a hoss
    And I'll show him who's boss
Unless, of coss, I take a fall.

THE BALLAD OF PAUL QUIXOTE

Sir Paul sat in his castle on top of the hill
And thought that retirement was less than a thrill.
The onset of leisure was spoiling his day
And he longed to hitch up and ride out to the fray.
But the dragons were all being slain by young knights
Who really monopolized all the good fights.
"Oh, what can I do" he complained to the King.
"I can't play second fiddle and you know I can't sing!"
"Well, there *is* a *mean* job — but what could be fitter?
Prepare to attack the ubiquitous litter!
Be wary — it lurks on each side of the way--
If you see a knave tossing it, just make him pay."
"Oh great!" said Sir Paul as he mounted his steed
And rode off to discover who'd done this foul deed.
The litter was out there in trashy profusion
But the litterers weren't, which made for confusion.
I might find a sheriff who will come at my bidding,
But the officer said, "Sir Paul, surely you're kidding.
There are dragons to slay, and my men are so few--
Have coffee with me — then I must say adieu."
Well, I'll write to the chieftains and lords of the land,
Said Sir Paul as he hopefully took pen in hand.
The letters flew forth, but it's likely that they
Are now part of the litter along Seltice Way.
These windmills are tricky — my sword is a mess
I think I would rather stay home and play chess,
But the garbage is rising and soon we can't see
All the beautiful mountains, or even a tree.
So rally 'round, citizens, this battle is dire--
Let's show off the glory of the Inland Empire!

SECOND CHANCE

The warden shows you out the door
And gives you shirt and pants.
He says, "You are a lucky man.
You have a second chance."

The doctor said, "I'm glad to say
You have another chance.
How timely that you had your stroke
So near an ambulance."

The lover's quarrel grew so hot
It threatened their romance.
Before he slammed the door he said,
"Let's give it one more chance."

Now chance is very risky stuff--
Hope can't survive unaided.
Get out and give it your best shot,
Bad luck can be evaded.

Go straight, avoid your crooked pals,
Good health means vigilance,
Have patience with your quarrelsome mate,
You'll cinch that second chance.

BALLAD OF THE IDAHO ALAMO

They came from Minnesota to grow pot in Idaho,
Two hippies with a mission who said progress has to go.
Their hero was Chief Joseph of the tribe of the Nez Perce,
For Joseph's lifestyle was above the capitalistic curse.
They got a job out picking weeds and tending to the goats.
They also tended to the seeds they'd hidden in their coats.
They settled in a little shack they called the Red Farm House,
Took all the plumbing out in back to serve the goats and cows.
Now our house is purified, they said, and settled down to grow
Twelve marijuana plants, and spread them out in their window.
This window looked out on the road where passersby could see
Cannabis fronds in that abode like a lush green Judas tree.
The local law descended then in righteous moral wrath
And took these hippies to the jail where they went on the warpath.
"You have no right to interfere, this still is freedom's land!
Our Alamo we'll fight right here — like Joseph, make our stand."
Ah, Joseph's tribe went on to woe, a victim of oppression.
We also lost the Alamo — what chance a pot obsession?
A tempest in a teapot? Yes, but life is ever thus.
There is no more a wilderness where we can just be us.

I PLANTED PANSIES

I planted pansies yesterday
Beneath the hawthorn tree.
Whenever I walk down the steps
Their faces smile at me.

SEASONS

Give me a song for the seasons
To warm me when nights are cold.
Sing of the summertime sunshine
That paints all the landscape with gold.
Or tell of the blossoms of springtime,
The fragrance of awakening earth,
Or the warm smoky smells of autumn--
There is really no end to the worth
Of a land that keeps growing and changing,
You don't need a calendar's chart,
You can smell, see and feel each new season
Remembering it well with your heart.

FOREVER SPRING

Spring comes in on winter's coattails
Scattering clouds of snow and mist,
Yet all her fearsome posturings
Must yield to Nature's calendar.
Soon the sun calls out the grass and flowers
And once again the ancient cycle
Stirs the world to life.

All this has happened without help from man,
That nosy denizen who fosters change
And cherishes false pride in powers of thought.
How long before he tries to challenge Nature's plan
And create pseudo springtime all the year?
A springtime of eternal youth and play.
How sad to miss the golden summer's ripening
And Autumn's gifts before the winter sleep.

PORTRAIT OF BERNICE

After the usual buffets of life
Old age should be gentle and kind
But she faces a future that's still full of strife
For she knows that she soon may be blind.

Her years as a teacher come back to her now
As she sits in her neat little flat
But her days and her nights aren't lonely somehow
She has Barney, her presumptuous cat.

Her humor and wisdom still brighten each day
And her friends know that they too are blest,
For her courage helps all of us seek out the way
To meet and to conquer life's test.

What gift can we give you at Christmas, my friend?
Our trinkets are of little worth,
For you are the giver, you teach to the end,
And leaven our days here on earth.

TO THE MOTHERS OF HANDICAPPED CHILDREN

I know where the Angels are.
They walk among us,
And when life deals out a hand
Too difficult to play,
God says, "I'll give to you
An Angel for a mother
So you will know I've not abandoned you."
Then the crumpled souls lift up
Within their damaged bodies
And they say, "Thank you, God,
For the wondrous gift of life."

CINDERELLA

Dreaming amid the ashes, awaiting their return,
She rests from their incredible demands.
"Come, comb my hair and wash my aching feet,
For we are dancing at the Prince's ball."
Their tongues' staccato jabs pierced her inadequacies.
And sent her scurrying to obey.
But now they are gone and the golden carriage waits
As the fairy godmother casts a final spell
To lend enchantment to the royal rendezvous.
Ah, Time, your magic made the years fly by--
Now Cinderella and her Prince reach toward the ever after.
On slippers of glass she totters toward his call,
"Ella, my dear, do bring my hassock and my pipe
And soothe my brow awhile before you sit
Once more beside my feet."

PANDORA'S BOX

The troubles we have in the world today
We can blame on a girl named Pandora
Who was sent down to earth with a box full of sins
To plague men, who found her adora-
ble, beautiful, sugar and spice
In spite of those vices (the mischief)
which was not quite so nice.
So when things look their blackest
And the men start to mope,
She'll reach into her box
And finesse them with Hope.

SECRET FRIEND

A teacher is a creature with a purpose here on Earth.
She restrains you, entertains you,
And helps you find your worth.
A student, never prudent, may often fall behind,
But she teaches you, beseeches you
To open up your mind.
Full measure of your pleasure may be many years away,
But the caring and the sharing
Are her gift to you today.

DISCOVERY

How strange to push the boundaries of thought
And find they are elastic.
They bounce you back beyond the starting point
To brand new revelations. A game!
A miracle! How wonderful it is
To stand upon a strange new premise
And leap again into the magic of the mind.

SENRYU

CHILDREN

Playing at life
  with dolls and trucks,
  They look toward the future--
And dream.

PARENTS

Caring for children,
  driving the trucks,
  They build the foundations
Of home.

ELDERS

Alone with memories,
  they cling to
  the empty carapace--
And dream.

GP

CHRISTMAS

At first a distant tinkle
Of a shaken harness bell
As little hooves pound closer.
Now everyone can tell
That Santa Claus is coming--
The sparks fly as he whirls,
Then climbs down every chimney
To reward good boys and girls.

CHILDREN

Children take you by the hand
And show you bugs and ants.
They peer intently at the flower
In strange reconnaisance.
They sometimes need to take apart
Those things that are a riddle,
The direct approach the only route--
They cross puddles in the middle.
We may think that we're the teachers,
But we too have much to learn
From childhood's wondrous view of life.
Through children we discern
That once for us the world was new.
Perhaps we should defer
To simple truths and answers
And find the child we were.

WHERE IS THE MISTLETOE?

My mommy says I should be good
For Santa's on his way.
I didn't mean to tease the cat,
But he didn't want to play.
So then I took the kettles out
And left them on the floor
And Daddy almost broke his neck
When he came in the door.
I accidentally broke Sue's doll--
Her head was always loose,
But Sue said that I killed her
With a nasty hangman's noose.
Well, now nobody loves me,
And there's no place left to go.
I think I need a little kiss--
Where is the mistletoe?

COME BACK TO BETHLEHEM

Come back to Bethlehem
When Christmas was a star.
No need to fear its bright clear rays
That spread its message far.
It promised love and lasting peace,
Joy, good will to all--
That simple message brought us hope
Why don't we heed its call?

Come back to Bethlehem,
Back to a better day.
Let Christmas hail the dawn of peace
Let terror fade away.
Oh, shining star, speak now of peace
And touch the hearts of men
Let your clear light show us the way
To Christmas once again.

FOR NICOLA JANE

Each time I say goodnight to you, my sweet,
I say goodbye to the child you were today.
Perhaps these little partings help to meet
The day you spread your wings and fly away.
Yet each goodbye is really a sweet sorrow
For I can hardly wait, my pet, to greet
The new, enchanting child you'll be tomorrow.

TEDDY POLTERGEIST

Little Teddy Poltergeist
Sings a little song.
Lights go on if they are off
And out if they are on.

He talks of looking for a ghost,
Yet seems about to flee
If Mommy can't be found at once
He howls like a banshee.

His wishes are the word of law--
It's hard to reconcile
His stormy frowns and gestures
With the sweetness of his smile.

When Teddy comes into a room
Things fly around it's true,
And if you are not agile
His trucks will clobber you.

Oh Teddy Poltergeist is three--
And sings his little song,
Knowing that the world is his
For he can do no wrong.

ESSENCE

The ancients looked for absolutes
and searched for final answers
to the mystery of Life.
As they gathered in the square
each day beneath the trees,
Truth was balanced on the scale
And Beauty failed the test of time.
Is this all there is? they asked each other,
not knowing they were coining a cliche.
They could have asked the women
who saw Truth in childhood's eyes
and knew the essence of all Life
is captured briefly in a baby's smile.

ON OUR FORTIETH

When two hearts come together
At first there's a flash
And the certainty that this is Fate
But the journey in tandem
Has altered our courses
And turned us each into a mate.
One says, "I am me!"
"No, you're not -- I am me!"
Until a new course appears
And the journey together
Has turned into one
That has lasted for forty long years.

VALENTINE

This valentine I give to you today
Is different from the ones of yesterday.
It speaks of patience learned throughout the years,
Of love that has been tested, and of tears.
Youth's passion once so easily declared
Is melded now into a lifetime shared.
And everything you are becomes more clear
As Valentine's Day adds another year.

VALENTINE #43

Marriage is such a momentous occasion.
You have no idea about the kids you'll be raisin',
To say nothing about whether your newly-wed mate
Has habits that you can at least tolerate.
Can he handle the crises that often arise?
Can she keep him still thinking that he's in Paradise?
It's always a gamble when two become one--
I'm glad we found laughter and times that were fun.
Fate took a hand on the day that we met
And our Valentine vows are sustaining us yet.
We brought up a family that deserves an ovation
And now we're at work on the next generation
Have the years told you truly our love's here to stay--
That you are my knight who keeps dragons away?
Those forty-three years call for an encore--
Shall we go for another to make forty-four?

TO MY VALENTINE

For 16 years you have been mine
So you must be my Valentine.
Though many things have come to vex us
You're still the guy I wed in Texas--
The one who promised to be true
And that is why I still love you.

GP